CLEVELAND INDIANS

JODY BRANNON

CREATIVE EDUCATION

Double play! Mike Hargrove, one of the rough, tough modern-day Indians, goes for two in 1981 action.

Library of Congress Cataloging in Publication Data

Brannon, Jody.
   Cleveland Indians.

   Summary: A history of Cleveland's "Tribe" from the beginning years in the 1880's, through the championship 1940's, to the aspirations for another pennant in the 1980's.
   1. Cleveland Indians (Baseball team)—History—Juvenile literature.   [1. Cleveland Indians (Baseball team)—History.   2. Baseball—History]
I. Title.
GV875.C7B72   1982   796.357'64'0977132   82-14917
ISBN 0-87191-859-5

CLEVELAND INDIANS

Cleveland is a whole lot more than just the largest city in Ohio. It's also the home of some of the world's most loyal and patient fans.

Cleveland has fielded a pro baseball team since 1869, the first year of organized pro ball. Over the years, the Forest Citys, Spiders, Blues, Bronchos, Naps and Indians have entertained millions of cheering fans.

The Indians, as the team has been called since 1915, have responded to the hometown support by bringing three pennants and two world championships to the bustling midwest city, located on the southern shore of giant Lake Erie.

Many exciting players have starred for the Tribe— from Hall-of-Famers such as Napolean Lajoie, Tris Speaker, Cy Young, Bob Feller, Bob Lemon and Satchel Paige to modern-day standouts like Bert Blyleven, Mike Hargrove, Toby Harrah, Bake McBride and Andre Thornton.

The Indians of the 1980s promise to bring as much fireworks to Cleveland Stadium, as the old Cleveland Forest Citys did over a century ago.

CLEVELAND BASEBALL IN THE HORSE-AND-BUGGY DAYS

The history of pro baseball in Cleveland begins with the Forest Citys in 1869. During those early days, the

The immortal Nap Lajoie shows the form that gave him a lifetime batting average of .339

TAKE ANOTHER BASE, MIKE
Mike Hargrove, who was the 1974 American League Rookie of the Year while wearing the uniform of the Texas Rangers, came to Cleveland in 1979. A year later he earned 111 bases on balls—a mark which ranks him third on the American League's all-time walk list.

7

THE FIRST NUMBER
Cleveland's Jack Graney may never be elected to the Hall of Fame for his baseball skills, but he will be remembered for something else. On June 26, 1916, Graney became the first player to wear a number on his uniform.

game was marked by hard hitting and sloppy fielding. Teams sometimes ran up scores such as 86-8 or 45-9. In a split doubleheader between Cleveland and the (N.Y.) Haymakers, the two clubs knocked in a total of 109 runs! Another game was believed to have been called in the sixth inning because the scorekeeper had collapsed from exhaustion. After only five innings, Cleveland was ahead 132-1. You can bet that those who bought the $10 season tickets and drove their buggies right up to the baselines got their fair share of scoring action.

Of course the early Cleveland teams didn't win all their games. In fact, they usually finished in the middle of the pack.

"They look awful," moaned the owner of the 1888 team as his players fumbled grounders. "All skinny and spindly. They're nothing more than spiders. Might as well call this team the Spiders and be done with it."

Even with their new name, the Cleveland Spiders didn't really play very well.

In 1890, however, their fortunes took a turn for the better when the team signed a 23-year-old farmboy to a $75 per month contract.

Denton True Young stomped eagerly to the mound on August 6 to face the Chicago Colts and their fierce batting champ, Cap Anson. It was Young's first big-league game. Anson called Young "just another big farmer," which made Denton hopping mad. That afternoon Young

Denton "Cy" Young may have been the greatest pitcher who ever lived. Baseball's highest pitching award is named after him.

buried the Colts in a maze of fastballs to secure a 3-1 Cleveland victory. He made Anson eat his words by striking him out. Despite the win, Young was disturbed after the game.

"I didn't have my usual speed today," he complained. His teammates were surprised by his gripe: "We thought you did. What happened?"

"Well, down in Canton," Young said, referring to his local minor-league club, "the catchers couldn't hold me, I was so fast. But Chief Zimmer had no trouble today, so I guess I didn't have much speed," he shrugged.

His new friends laughed, "That's a compliment to Zimmer," explained one man. "The Chief is the best catcher in the league, not one of those fellows who couldn't hold you in Canton."

Young who had impressed more than just his teammates, was soon pegged "Cyclone", because of his awesome pitching velocity.

Today, each time Cleveland fans hear the name Cy Young, they are filled with pride. The Cy Young award, major-league baseball's annual award for the best pitcher in baseball, is named in his honor. Young was the man who almost single-handedly taught the world that pitching alone could win ballgames.

In his short rookie season, Young picked up 10 victories against seven defeats. The next year, he ran up a

Cy Young in action. He won more games (511) than any other hurler.

BASEBALL'S FIRST PERFECTO *On June 12, 1880, the Old Cleveland Forest Citys were playing Worchester, Massachusetts and facing John Lee Richmond, a right-handed pitcher. Richmond won the game by retiring 27 consecutive Cleveland batters to become the first man to hurl a perfect game.*

27-22 record, although the club finished a disappointing fifth.

In 1892, the team went 53-23 behind Young's amazing 35-10 record, pushing their way into the first world championship. Unfortunately, they met the Boston Beaneaters, the game's most powerful and popular franchise. The Beaneaters swept the best-of-nine series.

Over the next few years, even Cy Young's pitching wasn't quite enough to spark the Spiders into the play-offs again. But in 1895 he lead his team into the Temple Cup, the old-time version of the World Series. Young defeated the rowdy Baltimore Orioles for three of Clevelands' four Series victories. The Spiders waltzed away with the special Temple Cup and an extra $528 each.

THE ONE-AND-ONLY NAP LAJOIE

By the winter of 1900, Cleveland was without a baseball team. The Spiders had compiled the world's worst season record by winning only 20 games and losing 134. They had disbanded in embarrassment.

Fortunately, a small group of ambitious men convinced a Cleveland bank president to build a new team for the baseball-hungry city. In 1901, the team was known as the Blues because they still wore the old blue uniforms of the Spiders. In 1902, the club was renamed the Bronchos, a name symbolic of power and strength.

Biting fastball. Bert Blyleven was traded to the Indians in 1981. He likes his new home.

Perhaps the best player to star for the Bronchos was a man who forced yet another name change for the club in 1903. In his first four years in the majors, 1897-1900, Napoleon Lajoie had hit .363, .328, .379 and .346 for the Philadelphia Phillies of the National League. In 1901, the Philadelphia A's of the new American League, offered Napoleon more money, and he accepted their offer. The Phillies sued and Lajoie was forbidden by a court order to play for any team in Pennsylvania except the Phillies. So Lajoie was traded to Cleveland.

When Lajoie donned his Broncho uniform, the Cleveland squad was in last place. Over the next few months, however, Napoleon swatted .369, Charley Hickman batted .363 and Bill Bernhard, who had come to town in the same deal with Lajoie, compiled the league's best mound record (18-5). It was good enough for a respectable fifth place finish.

Napoleon became team captain. Later, he was honored again when the team name was changed to the "Naps" after a city-wide contest.

Cleveland was now picked to win the 1903 pennant, and the fans were anxious to help. In one game the crowd was so enthusiastic that spectators spilled onto the field and prevented the game from continuing until the players joined hands in a human chain and pushed the fans back into the stands. The Naps finished third for the year.

Hard luck. Len Barker had a no-hitter going in this 1980 contest against the Yanks, but lost it in the late innings.

TOBACCO SPITTER
Napoleon Lajoie was the sixth player admitted to the Hall of Fame. Remembered for his enthusiastic play on the field, Lajoie sometimes got carried away in the excitement. "If he didn't like an umpire's call," recalled one fan, "he'd give him a face full of tobacco juice."

15

Despite an abundance of talent, the 1904 Naps found themselves in fifth place when manager William Armour resigned. Napolean became player/manager and directed the team into fourth place.

The next summer the club was again billed as pennant contenders, but an injury to Lajoie squelched their title hopes. Napolean was spiked in a routine play at second but continued to play since the wound didn't seem too severe. The dye from his socks infected the cut, which kept him out of the lineup for two months. The team dropped out of the race and lost the favor of the fans. On September 5, only 224 people showed up to watch a ballgame.

Lajoie played for Cleveland from 1902 to 1914, During that period, he was joined by several Cleveland standouts. Adrian C. "Addie" Joss, the well-liked ironman hurler, is just one example. In 1908, Addie got off to a superb start, accounting for nine of the team's first 15 victories. He won nine of his first ten games, and he walked only four batters in his first nine decisions!

On October 2, 1908, Addie was on the mound against the Chicago White Sox in a crucial battle during the pennant stretch. Joss was hot. Inning after inning, his famous fadeaway pitch had taken a deadly toll on the Sox batters. Finally, Addie found himself facing pinch-hitter John Anderson in the top of the ninth, with two

At the turn of the century, Addie Joss was busy earning a place in the Baseball Hall of Fame.

16

outs. Cleveland led 1-0. If Addie could only get Anderson for the final out, he would become the sixth pitcher in baseball history to toss a perfect game.

He did.

Despite Joss' chilling performance, the Naps missed the pennant by a half-game, finishing .004 behind the Detroit Tigers. Joss, who was respected for his gentlemanly behavior both on and off the field, vowed: "Things will be different next year."

In 1909, Cy Young (who had been traded in 1898) returned to a Cleveland uniform in a deal with the Red Sox. Boston's manager thought the 42-year old great was over the hill, but Cy proved him wrong by wrapping up 19 victories for Cleveland. Sadly, those were among the few games the team won all year. Cleveland sportswriters became disgusted with the home-town team.

"Naps?" laughed one. "They ought to be known as the Napkins, the way they fold up." Cleveland finished sixth that year, 27½ games out of first. Napoleon Lajoie resigned his managerial duties and hung up his uniform.

THE TRIBE TAKES OVER

With Nap no longer at the helm, a contest was held to select a new team name. From now on, the team would be known as the Cleveland Indians, or simply the "Tribe."

The arrival of one of the all-time best centerfielders,

Tris Speaker led the Indians to a World Championship in 1920, and proved himself one of the all-time great outfielders.

THE ALL-TIME BEST INDIANS In 1969, the Cleveland fans selected the following players as their all-time favorite stars at each position: Hal Trosky, first base; Napoleon Lajoie, second base; Lou Boudreau, shortstop; Ken Keltner, third base; Steve O'Neill, catcher; Charley Jamieson, left field; Tris Speaker, center; Joe Jackson, right; Bob Feller, right-handed pitcher; and Vean Gregg, left-handed pitcher.

When Napoleon Lajoie retired from the Cleveland squad in 1914, the Naps looked for a new name for the team. A local newspaper held a contest and the name "Indians" was recommended by a fan who said he was suggesting it in honor of Luis Francis "Chief" Sockalexis, who was the first Indian to play in the big leagues. He played for the Clevelanders for three seasons in the late 1890s.

Tristan Speaker, in 1916 marked the beginning of a winning tradition for the Indians. The hot-headed Texas cowboy had been traded by the Boston Reds to Cleveland for $55,000 and two players.

Speaker, 28, quickly adapted to his new baseball park. He liked the closeness of the right-field wall, only 290 feet from home plate.

"It was as natural for me to try to hit that wall, as it would be for any batter," smiled Tristan. "You try to take advantage of the style of your home field." With that, the mighty left-hander swatted a hefty .386 to unseat the legendary Ty Cobb as the American League batting champ. Cobb, who had held the crown for nine straight years, was doubly upset about losing the award because he knew Speaker was also a better outfielder. He was surehanded, speedy and graceful—all qualities Cobb was short on.

With Speaker in the line-up, the Indians finished in sixth place, only 14 games out of first with a 77-77 record. That was quite a turn-around from their disgraceful 1915 seventh-place record of 57-95—44½ games off the pace!

Steadily, now, the Indians crept into the pennant picture. In 1917, they finished third; the next two years, they placed second. Then, in the middle of the 1919 season, Speaker was selected to be the new Cleveland manager.

In 1954 Bobby Avila launched himself to the top of the American League with a .384 batting average. He connects here for a single.

THE 1920 WORLD CHAMPIONSHIP

On August 16, 1920, Cleveland visited the Yankees at the Polo Grounds. It was Speaker's first full season as Manager. His best friend, Indian shortstop Ray Chapman, stepped to the plate in the first inning. Chapman was facing New York pitcher Carl Mays, who was called a "submarine twirler" because of his sweeping underhand delivery.

As Speaker watched from the dugout, something horrible happened.

"Mays tossed an inshoot that seemed to hypnotize Chapman," recalled a sportswriter, "It struck him on the temple, fracturing his skull and paralyzing the vocal chords, making it impossible for him to talk."

Chappie crumpled in the batter's box. He was rushed to the hospital for emergency brain surgery, but the beanball had taken its toll. Chapman died early the next morning.

"He was the best friend I had," Speaker said softly of the good-natured hard-working infielder. Inspired by Chapman's memory, Cleveland rallied behind the pitching of Jim Bagby who, with his 31-12 record, joined Cy Young as the only two single-season 30-game winners in Cleveland history.

Cleveland went on to win 98 games that year—more than enough for the American League Pennant. Heading

Cleveland third baseman Al Rosen could hit, run and score. A slide by Rosen beat Detroit in this 1950 night game.

GEORGE BURNS, FIRST MVP
In 1926, George Burns became the first Indian ever to win the American League's MVP award. Although he had a funny batting stance—he insisted on keeping his feet close together—Burns swatted 64 doubles for a major-league record and earned a .358 batting average. Lou Boudreau (1948) and Al Rosen (1953) are the other two Tribesmen to win the award.

into the World Series against the rugged Brooklyn Dodgers, the Indians were actually favored to win. The entire city of Cleveland was numb with excitement. Shops closed down. Tickets were as valuable as gold.

The best-of-nine Series was deadlocked at two games each when Speaker named Bagby as the starter for the fifth game. Little did Speaker realize that this particular contest would stand out in the record books forever.

In the first inning, the Tribe loaded the bases. Wiry Elmer Smith stepped to the plate and slammed a 1-2 pitch over the right-field bleachers to become the first man to hit a grand slam in World Series play.

In the fourth inning, Bagby was at bat with two men on. He, too, swatted a homer, thus becoming the first pitcher in Series history to club a four-bagger. The Indians now led, 7-0.

Wait, there's more. The Dodgers had men on first and second when Clarence Mitchell nailed a liner to Cleveland second baseman Bill Wambsganss. Wamby snagged the ball, skipped over to double the runner up at second and tagged the player from first for an unassisted triple play—another World Series first!

In the end, of course, the red-hot Indians took it all. For the first time in history, Cleveland was named world champs. For their heroics, the players pocketed a cool $4,204 apiece.

Pitcher Mike Garcia had a lot to smile about in 1949. The Tribe was coming off a world championship.

The following year the Indians played hard in hopes of returning to the 1921 World Series, but the Yankees outlasted them. It would be many years before the Indians would once again wear the insignia of baseball's World Champions.

YOUNG BOB FELLER

"Gentlemen, I've found the greatest young pitcher I ever saw," reported Cleveland team executive Cy Slapnicka at a private luncheon in 1936. "I suppose this sounds like the same old stuff to you, but I want you to believe me. This boy that I found out in Iowa will be the greatest pitcher the world has ever known. I only saw him pitch once before I signed him."

The board of directors were bubbling with curiosity about 16-year-old pitching sensation, Bob Feller.

"Bob's finishing out his school term," explained Slapnicka, "but I repeat to you gentlemen, he will be the star of them all. Do you know that he averaged 19 strikeouts a game last summer?"

A few weeks later, Feller took the mound for Cleveland in St. Louis. The Cardinals had legendary guys like Frankie Frisch, Leo Durocher, Joe Mediwick, Pepper Martin and Dizzy and Paul Dean. Feller threw the middle three innings. The Tribe's manager, Steve O'Neill, was his catcher for two of his three-frame stint.

The amazing Bob Feller is enshrined in the Baseball Hall of Fame.

FAST FELLA, THAT FELLER
The great Bob Feller collected three career no-hitters and 12 one-hitters. His wicked fastball was once clocked at 98.6 mph. "At that rate of speed," Feller explained, "it took about one-third of a second for the ball to leave my fingers and get up to the plate."

*LEGENDARY
NUMBERS
Of the 18
numbers which
have been
permanently
retired from the
American
League, three
numbers be-
longed to
Cleveland greats.
They are Bob
Feller (19), Lou
Boudreau (5)
and Earl Averill (3).*

"That kid's too tough for me to catch any more," complained O'Neill while rubbing his bruised palm and watching another catcher strap on the protective gear. "He throws that thing so fast it looks like a pea."

Hurling nothing but fastballs, Feller fanned eight of the nine Cardinals he faced. After the game, a photographer asked Dizzy Dean if he'd pose with the shy young pitcher for a few shots. "Why ask me?" Dizzy retorted. "Ask the kid if he'll pose with me!"

Feller went on to strike out 15 batters in his official major-league debut, defeating St. Louis on August 23, 1936. A few weeks later he matched Dizzy Dean's big-league strikeout record by fanning 17 Philadelphia A's.

All across the nation people marveled at young Feller. But somehow the Tribe couldn't muster a pennant-winning effort until 1940. By this time, Feller was a strong five-year veteran who was expected to lead the Tribe to the pennant. He set out to do just that.

The 1940 Opening Day temperature hovered in the thirties, but the cold air didn't bother Feller and his fireball. He easily mowed down the White Sox, thus becoming the first man to pitch a no-hitter on Opening Day.

LOU BOUDREAU
THE YOUNGEST MAJOR LEAGUE MANAGER

As the Indians roared through the 1940's, there came a time when they had to pause to hire a new manager.

Lou Boudreau hits the deck. It was this kind of hustle that made the Indians world champs in 1948.

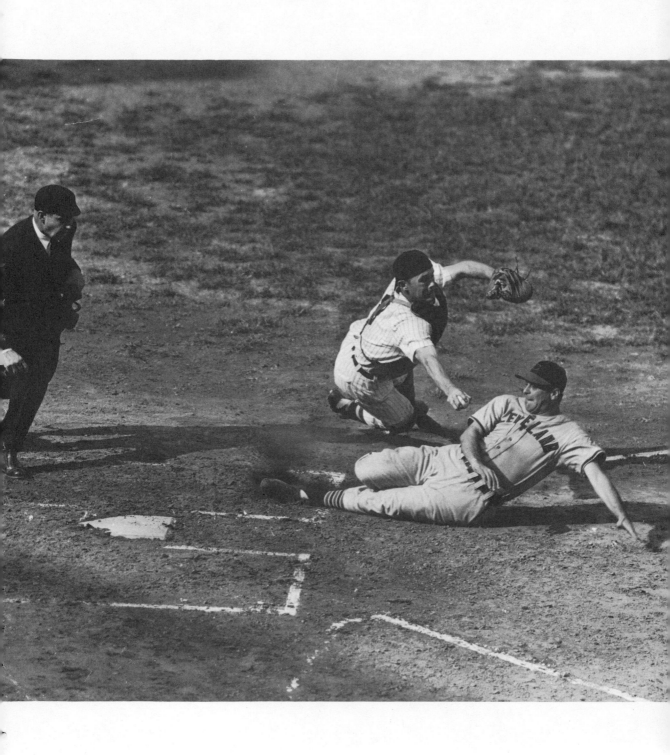

Someone suggested 24-year-old Lou Boudreau, the two-year veteran shortstop. "He's practically been the manager all along," reasoned one of the team's directors. "Besides, he's been the captain or leader on every team he's played on."

Alva Bradley, the Cleveland owner, wasn't so sure. "Boudreau is the greatest shortstop in the world," sighed Alva. "I'm not going to ruin his career by burdening him with the problems of managing. I think he's too young."

Alva finally gave in, and Boudreau became the youngest man to skipper a major-league team.

Sadly, Boudreau never got a chance to become the youngest to guide a team into the World Series. With the outbreak of World War II, most of his stars were called into the service of Uncle Sam.

After the war, Bill Veeck, a rich young businessman, purchased the team and set about making it a hit. Veek had a motto for the club: "Every day is Mardi Gras and every fan is a king." He made coming to the ballpark fun. He hired a comedian who would hit pitches while hanging by his knees from a portable trapeze, and who wore a snake for a belt. Veeck organized cow-milking competitions between the players. He let everyone into the last game of the season for free. He announced "A night for the greatest shortstop ever left off the All-Star Team" to honor manager Lou Boudreau. He signed Larry Doby to a contract which made the American League's first black player.

Big Andre Thornton tries to stretch a triple into a homer in 1981 action against the Angels.

MORE THAN A SLUGGER
Andre Thornton has won several awards during his long career, especially during the years he has played for the Indians. In 1979, Andre was named the ninth annual Roberto Clemente Award winner, recognizing his humanitarianism and contributions to baseball.

THE 1948 PENNANT RACE

In 1948, Cleveland was equipped to be a pennant winner. Boudreau was determined, and his players were willing to sweat. By working hard at the training camp, the Tribe got off to a fast start. They won their first six games and were leading the division on June 30, much to the amazement of the other teams. "Don't worry about the Indians," said the Philadelphia coach. "They'll fall apart, they always do."

Veeck and Boudreau were determined not to let that happen. They had already transformed Bob Lemon, a medicore outfielder, into an awesome pitcher (Lemon would no-hit Detroit on his way to a 20-14 record that year.) All they needed was one more spark in the pitching corps. Veeck reached deep into the minor leagues and pulled out a wily old veteran who was somewhere between the ages of 45 and 65 when he finally stepped onto the big-league mound. Old Satchel Paige, the ageless wonder, reached his long-time dream on July 7, by finally becoming a major-league hurler.

On August 8, the Tribe found itself in the heat of the pennant race. Battling each other for the championship, the Indians, A's and Yankees were separated by only two percentage points the day the Tribe entertained the Yanks in a twin bill before a huge crowd of 73,484.

With the score 6-4 New York in the seventh frame of the first game, Boudreau knew he needed a pinch-hitter

Cleveland third baseman Bob Lemon hits the deck against the Cards in 1931. Lemon would continue his great career as manager of the Yankees.

to spark his team. He finally decided that he would send himself into the line-up to do the honors.

With his heart beating wildly, Boudreau fumbled for a bat and strode gamely into the batter's box. He tapped the plate a few times...took a deep breath...and rapped a hard liner to center, knocking in two runs to knot the score. The Indians went on to wrap up the game and the nightcap, too.

Now, Boudreau's team was inspired. On August 15, Feller blanked the White Sox. The following day Lemon blanked the same team, 8-0. Then Gene Bearden beat the Browns 8-0. Sam Zoldak shut out St. Louis, 3-0, and Paige egged the White Sox, 1-0. When Lemon took the mound on August 21, Cleveland pitchers had not allowed a run in 39 straight innings. Eight scoreless innings later, Lemon had shattered the American League record of 41 innings (estabished by the Cleveland Blues in 1903) and set the new mark at 47.

But the season's real hero turned out to be Boudreau who hit .355 and was named Most Valuable Player in leading the Tribe to the verge of the 1948 pennant. To capture the title, however, Cleveland first had to deal with the Boston Red Sox in a chilling American League playoff game. Here's what happened:

Boudreau looked over his pitching staff. There was Feller, Lemon, Paige, Bearden...Who should he pencil in as the starting pitcher for this crucial game?

Lou leaned toward Bearden, but he decided to ask the team its opinion.

The legendary Satchel Paige hams it up in 1948. Satch was still playing big league ball in his 50's.

THE ANCIENT MOUNDSMAN *Satchel Paige was old enough to be a grandfather when he made his first major league appearance in 1948. Although some guessed he was at least 50 years old, Paige earned a 6-1 record and his 2.48 ERA was second best in the league that year.*

"We've gone along with you all season, Lou," said one player. "I think we'd be crazy not to go along with you for this big one." His teammates agreed.

Bearden won the game, but it was Boudreau himself who carried the action. In the first inning, Lou homered. In the fourth, he singled. In the fifth, he nailed another fourbagger. In the ninth, he singled. He also drew an intentional walk. The result? The Indians clinched their second pennant of all time with an easy 8-3 victory.

WORLD CHAMPS!

The Milwaukee Braves were next. The Brave's Johnny Sain, a 24-9 winner, outlasted Feller in the opening game. The next day Lemon bounced back to tie the series.

Bearden and Steve Gromek came through with Cleveland decisions in games three and four to give the Tribe a 3-1 series lead.

More than 86,200 people came to watch Feller, a long-time sentimental favorite, polish off the Braves, but Cleveland was crushed in that fifth game, 11-5.

In the sixth contest, Lemon was tapped again as the pitcher, and he did exactly what Feller had wanted to do: Bring the world crown to Cleveland.

No one was prouder than Lou Boudreau. From the very first day of spring training he'd sensed that his job was on the line. He had to win the pennant.

In the unforgettable 1948 season, guys like Gene Bearden (left) and Ken Keltner led the way.

"Nobody knew better than I did that my job as manager of the Indians hung on the outcome of that play-off game. I was convinced Veeck was ready to trade me or buy up my contract as manager if we didn't win the pennant." But Lou came through.

"Lou was determined to prove I was a jerk," Veeck grinned. "I was. He did. So he was the champ, and he gets a new contract."

Lou hoped to lead the team back to the Series in 1949, but the old Indian jinx took hold again. They slipped to third, then fourth in 1950.

In 1951 Al Lopez became the new skipper. For three straight years the Tribe finished a frustrating second.

Then came 1954, and another stunning record. By compiling a regular season mark of 111 wins against 43 defeats, the Indians eclipsed the previous record of 110 victories, set by the mighty 1927 Yankees.

The 1954 Cleveland pitching staff was clearly the best in baseball. Bob Lemon and Early Wynn each own 23 games. Mike Garcia went 19-8. Bob Feller, at age 35 and in his 19th major-league season, was 13-3. The pitching was supported by super fielding and defense. Unfortunately, the team had only two .300 hitters—Bobby Avila and Al Rosen.

Nevertheless, Cleveland waltzed confidently into the World Series to meet the New York Giants. Maybe the Indians were too confident. Maybe the Giants were

RED-HOT ROOKIE In 1933, the super rookie was Hal Trosky, a first baseman. Trosky drove in 142 runs and earned a .330 average in his first pro campaign. His totals for doubles, total bases and homers still stand as rookie records.

Out by a foot. Oakland's Dick Green is nailed by Chris Chambliss, the 1971 Rookie of the Year.

still sky-high from their exciting National League playoff victory over thier arch-foes, the Brooklyn Dodgers. Though Cleveland came out howling, the Giants easily swept the Series.

THE POST-PENNANT YEARS

Since 1957, Cleveland had finished better than third only once. With three exceptions, they have ended each season at least 14 games out of the pennant picture. Despite the disappointing seasons, several exciting stars have worn the Cleveland colors.

Rocky Colavito, a power-hitting centerfielder for the Indians for eight summers, was voted by the fans in a 1969 tally as the "Most Memorable Personality." Rocky shares the team record for most homers in a month with Hal Trosky (13). He also holds the Indians record for most home runs by a right fielder with 42 which he swatted in 1959.

First baseman Chris Chambliss waltzed away with the 1971 Rookie of the Year award by slugging nine homers and 48 RBI for a .275 batting mark. He played for Cleveland for four seasons.

"Sudden" Sam McDowell wore a Cleveland uniform in six All-Star games. He is the second best strikeout artist in Cleveland history with 2,281, only 300 behind Feller's career total. Feller compiled his mark in 17½ seasons while McDowell reached his in only 10.

Most Memorable Personality. That's the honor bestowed on Rocky Colavito by Cleveland fans.

In 1972, Gaylord Perry, the notorious spitballer became the only Indian ever to win the Cy Young award with his 24-16 record.

SUPER JOE

But perhaps the brightest rookie star to wear a Cleveland uniform was "Super" Joe Charboneau, the 1980 Rookie of the Year.

Charboneau had come a long way since he bought his first baseball glove with Blue Chip stamps and his first pair of cleats with money he earned by selling frogs for a quarter a piece.

In 1978, Cleveland management read a scouting report on the stocky young kid. "Charboneau has a compact but powerful swing. His arm is still below average and his speed ordinary. He's a hothead and doesn't always give 100 percent. A big-league hitter." Still, the scouts liked Joe's potential and worked a trade with the Phillies.

"I knew it was a break for me just to get to another organization that wanted me enough to trade for me," said Joe. "I knew that Cleveland hadn't done that well, and I figured I could help them."

But Joe knew even less about his team than he thought.

"Charboneau had no concept of the Indians history. He wasn't aware of Cleveland's deplorable past, or its

Gaylord Perry had a secret. After each pitch, he refused to take the ball back from the catcher until his mind was ready for the next pitch.

DESIGNATED TEAM GAMBLER **The Naps owners were counting on ticket sales for a 1905 weekend doubleheader to bring in enough money so the team could pay $1600 in overdue debts. When the games were rained out, pitcher Dusty Rhodes entered a card game, got hot and won $1,800— more than enough to pay the team's bills.**

43

***CHARBONEAU'S
BOOMER***
*As an Indian
rookie in 1980,
Joe Charboneau
hammered a
three-and-one
Tom Underwood
fastball almost
600 feet into the
third deck of
Yankee Stadium.
"It is a weird
feeling when you
hit a ball that
well," Joe grinned,
"you are numb,
floating on air."*

incredible hunger for a hero or a winner," wrote a baseball historian.

All Joe knew was that he was given a shot at the big leagues. During spring training he poured all his energy into improving his hitting and fielding. Like all rookies, he worried about being sent to the minors.

Rod Carew, the great hitting star, watched the hot young prospect during an exhibition game and predicted Joe would be the American League's top rookie.

"I did not find out I had made the team until three days before the start of the season," Joe recalls. "I was lying on the trainer's table and (coach Dave) Garcia walked in and told me I would be starting in left field for the opener against the Angels. I was terrified."

"Baseball is really strange," Joe continues. "I spent all spring worrying that I would hear that they cleaned out my locker. That is the sign you've been cut. Then all of a sudden I was a starter and batting cleanup."

Although Charboneau batted seventh for the opener, he was a big part of the lineup all season. He finished his rookie campaign with 23 homers, 87 RBI and a .289 batting average while leading Cleveland to only its second winning season in 11 summers.

The following year—1981—Joe's world turned upside down. An injury and a big slump sent him back to the minors. "I went from the Hall of Fame to the Hall of Shame," he recalls. "I worked my heart out to make it

Super Joe Charboneau was A.L. Rookie of the year in 1980, but was sent back to the minors with back problems. Here, he begins a comeback at spring training, 1982.

back on the team in 1982." By mid-season, however, Super Joe had been cut again.

THE FUTURE LOOKS GOOD

The Tribe of the 80's has potential. Lots of it. Some say that the pitching corps of Len Barker, John Denny, Rick Waits, Larry Sorenson and Bert Blyleven rated with the super hurlers of the '50s—Mike Garcia, Early Wynn, Bob Lemon, Bob Feller and Herb Score.

According to Cleveland insiders, major league veterans like Toby Harrah and Mike Hargrove will be brought in to anchor the fielding and provide batting punch and leadership for a growing group of eager stars who intend to bring another pennant to Cleveland Stadium soon.

Over the years, Cleveland fans have been patient and supportive. Quietly and steadily they have waited for a winning club to be constructed. Today's team thinks it has the necessary ingredients to be pennant winners. This particular Tribe is anxious to repay the loyal Cleveland fans with a World Championship banner. Baseball teams of both leagues take note. The Tribe is on the warpath.

Three straight shutouts. In 1981, John Denny blanked Seattle, Oakland and California in three starts.

HARGROVE "OLD FASHIONED" "Mike Hargrove could have played for any team in any era," explains Cleveland club President Gabe Paul. "You hate to say that anyone is old fashioned, but Mike is one of those guys who is a throwback to the past. He plays the game the way you are supposed to."

This pitch gave John Sorenson his first win as an Indian. Roaring into the
'82 season, Cleveland looked to youngsters like Sorenson to lead the way.